Midnight at Noon

Journey Johnson

Midnight at Noon

CONTENTS

DEDICATION	x
Forward by E. Nina Jay	1
1 One	6
First Earth	7
Either Way	9
Coffee	10
Orphans	11
Seaworthy	12
Twilight	14
Haystack	15
Saeed	17
Dark:30	18
2 Two	19
Juk	20
Vermont	23

| IV | –

Seasons	25
Memorex	27
Filter	28
Star	29
Pampered	31
Present Company Excluded	33
Maya	35
Spin Cycle	36
3 Three	38
Love Birds	39
Meshell	40
Dysmorphia	41
Wanderlust	42
Pretty	43
Th|ink	44
Psyche	45
Congo	46
Pilgrims	47
Samsara	48
4 Four	49
Impermanence	50
Solar	51

| Dawn 52
| Caterpillar 53
| Shift 54
| Seed 55
| Toni 56
| Zealot 57
| Alchemy 58
| Sanctuary 59
| ; 60
5 | Five 61
| Nocturne 62
| Celeste 63
| Evanescence 64
| Recyclable Souls 65
| Shadows 66
| Anima 68
| Undiagnosed 69
| Stutter 71
| Tea Time 72
6 | Six 73
| Poetry Be Lover 74
| The Sky is a Voyeur 77

| Lean Not | 79
| Basket | 81
| Familial | 83
| Indigenous | 84
| Sketch | 85
| Glue | 89
| 7 Seven | 92
| Splendid | 93
| Water Log | 94
| Hush | 95
| Flesh Envy | 96
| 8 Eight | 97
| Glitch | 98
| 40/Seven | 100
| lowercase gods | 102
| Send Them | 103
| Unreported | 104
| Armageddon | 105
| Surviving the Night | 107
| Courtship | 109
| Wake | 111
| 9 Nine | 112

| Fly | 113
| Salt | 114
| Billie | 116
| Orbit | 117
| Passport | 118
| Illusion | 119
| Old Shit | 120
| Night Sweats | 122
| Therapy | 124
| 10 | Ten | 126
| Rosario | 127
| Ku'ulei | 129
| Firefly | 130
| Noteworthy | 131
| Deserts | 133
| Gabriel | 134
| This Moment | 136
| Mercy | 138
| Reflection | 139
| 11 | Eleven | 140
| Beloved (For Toni) | 141
| See Unheard | 143

- Whitney 145
- Solace 146
- Forecast 147
- I Can 148
- Undistorted 150
- Wordlessness 151
- Misnomer 154
- The Gardener 155
- 12 Twelve 157
- Crush 158
- Is Love 159
- Songs II 160
- Lay Me Down 161
- Tempest 163
- Love Note 164
- Honey 166
- Prey 169
- Let 170
- Butterfly 171
- Dragonfly 172
- 12 173

Copyright © 2025 by Journey Johnson
All rights reserved. No part of this book may be reproduced in any manner whatsoever without written permission except in the case of brief quotations embodied in critical articles and reviews.
First Printing, 2025

> Healing begins where the wound was made.
> -Alice Walker

Forward by E. Nina Jay

Eye almost cried. Sat staring at the white. It was over. Eye knew eye could go back. Eye knew that. But still... this first time left me emoceanally saturated. Left me soaking wet and set on fire at the same time.

This is a splash. This is a moan. This is a roar.

Stepping out of these pages... eye felt it. It was like a first breakup of many. Eye didn't wanna leave. Poetic legs and arms still wrapped around my every sense.

Eye stumbled out of these pages drunkenly.
Crying and smiling. Naked and dancing.

Feeling seen in my ghetto crevices.
Feeling rubbed behind my ears when eye recognized ghosts.
Feeling loved in the nuances of black and human and womon and lesbian.
Feeling ethereal in a zoomed-out delicious.
Feeling inspired. Wanting to write and draw and paint and all while giggling.

Midnight reminds me how beautiful eye am. We all are. How exquisite it is to be walking through this human experience.

As eye gathered myself and my tears and closed the moments of my first Journey through Midnight, eye thought to myself what my body whispers since eye met this poet years ago...

> These are the kinds of poems
> That are gonna
> Save people
> Empower people
> Love people
> FREE people

And this culture/world needs this so deeply right now.

If you're reading this it means you are on your way into this magnificent being called a book.

> Open wide for it and let it
> work its way
> Softly through you.

E. Nina Jay

Midnight at Noon
Poems by
Journey Johnson

Copyright © 2025 by **Journey Johnson**
All rights reserved. No part of this publication may be reproduced, distributed or transmitted in any form or by any means, without prior written permission.

Publisher| **Verbanizm Ink**
Cover Design| **Journey Johnson**
Photo Credit| **Kim Roseberry**

Publisher's Note: This is a work of fiction. Names, characters, places, and incidents are a product of the author's imagination. Locales and public names are sometimes used for atmospheric purposes. Any resemblance to actual people, living or dead, or to businesses, companies, events, institutions, or locales is entirely coincidental.

Midnight at Noon/ Journey. –1st ed.
ISBN 978-0-9899300-31

One

First Earth

You were
    First God. Belly. Stretched
    Beyond. Brown horizon, I
Crawl over. And

My earth. Have
Mountains. I, cub
In cold world. Hibernate
Upon. Under. In
Safe

My earth. Eagle's wings
Of arms. Swoop down
Pick up, snatch from
Danger. Watch ground, I
From talons. My earth.
You were

First sky. Gaze be cloud
Cover. Stars twinkle when
God laugh. Overcast
Rain down. Thunder be
Threat in slide of eye

First heaven. You were
First religion. Born zealot
First church. Was hem
Of skirt. Pray under. Peek
Out. Grow up. Believe
In angels. Be sin
In saint.

My earth. You were
First God. Belly. Stretched
Beyond. Brown horizon, I
Walk into.

Either Way

What will happen is this
    You will fall in love
    You will run for your life
Or stand still in your courage
Or stupidity
Either way
You cannot outrun the train
Either way
You will become wreckage
Or Magic
Or both
Either way
You will
Fall
To pieces
And become
More
Or less
Your
Self
Either way.

Coffee

Sugar
    Is purest in the morning
        When the spiritual palate is clean.
    Before the sweat begins to bead.
    Before the eyes begin to sting.
    Before the fog of thought rolls in,
    Leaving its bitter cloud to
    Rain in your coffee.

Orphans

We speak
    Temporary tourniquets
        Into wounded moments
Lest our souls bleed out.

We are strugglest.
It's the struggle that strangles
Survival.

Hangs it from right winged
Left bird crashing into fraternal
Towers. Heaven

Is a bulletproof mosque
Surrounded by burning crosses
Drowning out sound of brailed prayers.

Salvation
Be the cursed verse of an illiterate scribe.
The scribble scrabble
Of an orphaned god.

Seaworthy

I would content myself
    To be the seaboard
        Over which your currents flow.

The sand
Beneath your breadth.
The earth third
Parted from your sun.

If to witness light
Only from the dark
And depth of your emotions
Be my surest source of sol,

Then in the shimmer
Of your shadows,
Conjure me

Immaculate
Phosphorescence.

Hold I, no temperament
Each time you reach for
Shore in shallow cove.

I am rock.
Secure,

I be source.
Every nuance of
En|tidal|ed stroke.

I am the
Course of crash.
I am the
Call of ebb.

And your flow
Is ever.. always
And eternal
Over me.

Twilight

We hang ourselves
      Upon a setting sun

Praying that tomorrow
Will rise to meet our feet.

That it is only the darkness
In the meanwhile
We must fear.

Haystack

With each
    Facade of a trial
    And inevitable
Not Guilty verdict
Over the lynching
Of our children,

I wonder
Is this the straw.
Is this the last
Motherfucking straw
That will finally break
The Black back.

Then. like clockwork
There comes another
And another and

The straws. Keep
Falling. Falling. Keep…

And then I see us
The needles. Eyes wide
And bulging in the noonday sun.

Black backs broken
Splayed. Captivating tapestry
In the pissy quilt of a slave hymn.

We cannot keep
Our eyes off ourselves. Dying

Long enough to
Find our way out.
Knuckles bloody
Necks arched

Throats stuffed with marching
Marching. Marching we are
Needles, baby. This
Is a haystack

Made of the marrow
Of Broken Black Backs.

Saeed

There is blood in our
    Apathy. shrapnel lodged in
    Our gluttony.

We are divided
By both-side-isms. There is
But one Goliath.

David is Saeed
And buried under rubble.
Name scribbled on chest

So those who find him
Will know to whom he belonged.
He belongs to us.

His body is ours
His blood is on our hands. His
Lineage ends here.

Inside these words. Outside
The blue birds sing as Gaza
Bleeds in the distance.

Dark:30

If we leave now
    We can catch our breath
    By morning

This barren space
Must not hold us
Hostage. Come,

Let us collect our souls
From windows faded by
Glare of a sun we have
Never had the courage
To look up to

Get up, lover
I cannot carry you
Not this time.

If we leave now
We can catch our breath
By morning.

Two

Juk

I knew a little boy once
    Folks called him Juk.
    His name was Pablo.

Pablo was an oddity
An enigma in the neighborhood.
Born to immigrants, he was seldom seen
Without his AC/DC baseball cap
And a stone in his right hand.

He rarely spoke more
Than a word or two on a string.
His shyness made him insecure.
Made him feel alien.

Pablo had one thing going for him,
His smile. Bright as a Lower East Side
Sunrise.

Now, this smile of his would
Draw the ladies. No words needed
Just smile for me, Pablo
And he did.

Inevitably Pablo would get
His signals crossed
Offer his heart and soul
To a bodega butterfly.

But Pablo was simple
And so instead of offering flowers

Or a date at the cinema,
He'd reach into his pocket
And pull out his stone. A token
Of love to his beloved.

Bad move.
Every time.
Pablo would lose
The love of his life
At least twice a week
In this manner.

Eventually, Pablo grew up
And out of his AC/DC cap.
Exchanged his tattered jeans
For slacks better complimenting
His button-down shirts.

But the stone,
He never outgrew the stone.
And never found a woman
Who'd take it, either.

So he let it rest there
In the shadows of his pockets
With the rest of his dreams.

Old man Juk, they called him.
Bought his own bodega some years back.
Crazy fool, the mamis would joke
Low-key dreaming they'd be the one
He finally bought flowers for.

One night Old Man Juk
Was wrapping up shop
When the bell above

TWO

The door chimed.

It was storming out
And she seemed to drag it in with her,
This silhouette of a goddess
Asking for prayer candles
And Nag Champa.

Flustered, Pablo vanished
Behind the beaded curtains,
Fetched a fresh batch of incense,
Smoothed his hair and tucked his shirt.

She waited
Quiet, seeing nothing in particular
Smelling of rain, sweet but
Somehow distant.

Pablo bagged the candles.
Wrapped the incense, smiled
His best Lower East Side sunrise,
Placed his precious stone
Inside the paper bag
And watched her
Walk away.

Vermont

The air raids sound.
    She steeps the tea.
        There is nowhere to go
That bombs cannot go also.

The window is open.
A sluggish breeze meanders
Through the kitchen.
It is 7 a.m. and already
The air hangs heavy.

She stands at the sink
Staring off into some other life
A million miles away from here.
America, maybe. Bombs
Never fall in Vermont.

It is autumn there
She is picking out apples
For pie. They love pie
In America.

Some hours from now
The adhan will echo from
The loudspeakers, but she
Will not pray. Where
Was God when her children
Were slaughtered?

Perhaps He, too, is dead.

Aha, these apples are perfect
She decides on her imaginary
Haul. She will take them
Home to her children.

In America, only leaves fall.
And so her children are alive.
Her husband, too, yes. Though
He doesn't beat her in Vermont.

Absentmindedly she sips
Her tea. It's gone cold. She
Sighs assessing the sky.
It is quiet. A cloudless blue.

Thank God, she thinks
Before remembering her life.
Before the tears roll from
Dry eyes. And so it is

God is dead.

Seasons

This is what they call them
    Segments of time
    And circumstance
Pockets of people
And bonds.

Beyond
These seasons
Only you can traverse
And even then
You will leave
Parts of yourself
Behind.

Sometimes
Only your very breath
Will make it through
To the other side.

You will have to start again
Either scratched
Or
From scratch

This is not to say
You will always lose people
Along the way.

No.

But believe this to be true,

The same way you will not be
Who you once were
Neither will they.

No one makes it
From one season to the next
Without changing or
Being changed.

I'll leave you with this
If you see me on the other side
Reintroduce yourself
And allow me to do the same.

Memorex

Some songs
    Will do that to you.

Snatch you from off-ramp
In the middle of rush hour
Traffic. There is no safety
In numbers.

No one notices
When it drags you through
Red light. Green. Back.

Shakes spirit from bone
Tightens skin over
Hollow of drum and
Beats you to the cadence

Of a memory you forgot
Somewhere along the way. Some
Songs will do that to you,

Make you dance to a rhythm
You thought you'd outrun.

Filter

Today
    I am walking through a field of orchids
        Planted over crime scenes
Never reported.

The sun
Is a familiar caress through the cool dew
Of petals fully aware of their seduction.

Only the chalked outlines of children
And the hum of muffled screams
Make the sway of beauty before me
Real enough to imagine.

Star

Old man
    It's hard to see star
        From incandescent city.

But I do
See you.

The way you
Shoot your self
Up

So high
So high

Can't touch you
Old man.

Can't see the stardust
In your cup
Milky Way in
Your cataracts.

Alley cat
Fell from Andromeda
Never we mind
Who you talkin' to.
Home folk hush
When blown smoke
Listen.

Old man

TWO

Turn dirty money
Into fire water.
Cardboard box
To equinox.
Be a bad motherfucker.

Slingshot soul
Tear hole like
Black bullet through
Black night.

Never see it comin'
Til it hit you
Up under
Blind light.

City life
Outshine star
When nightfall
S'why you stay high,
Old man.

So high
So high

Shoot self
Through intravenous
Sky.

I see you
Close eyes,
Make wish.

Pampered

We are
　　Domesticated opulence
　　Purring in the window
Of monotony.

We are
The envy of alley cats
Scavenging waste bin for
Scraps of discarded indulgence.
But my, how fierce they are
In their freedom.

We long
For fish eyes in the afternoon.
For the sting of spine
Caught in our throat.
To conquer nemesis
Twice our mass.

We hear
The clink of silver spoons.
Break spell of vicarious adventure.
Remember Serengeti
Of lives gone by.

Like slaves,
We jump from windowsill.
It is the nature of Stockholm
To wrap self 'round
Leg of master.

Swallow, we, the bitter tap.
Pretend it is river rushing over
Banks of captivity
Until is drowned, for now
The Lioness inside our belly.

Until silent
Is the roar beneath the purr
Of civil tongue
Just on other side
Of alley stray.

Present Company Excluded

I don't mind ghost
   Fact is
      I like the company.

But there came a point when
The house of my mind
Got too crowded
And I had to learn

To separate my own ghost
From Those left behind
By people who were careless
With their shit.

People who did not
Respect either of us enough
To take their belongings
With them when
The time came.

Once in a while
I'll notice one

Clung to my spirit
Like a child I
Did not born and
I'll say to it,

I have nothing against you
But you have to leave
I have my own mouths to feed.

And I'll hold the door open
With the tip of my pen
Until all that is left
Are the tracks of their feet
Across the mat of my page.

Maya

In time we find flesh
    And circumstance a phantasm.
      The company we keep keeps many faces
But the spirits are few.

Never confess to the shadows cast by a candle
What you can speak directly to the sun.
The flames may seduce but the flickers signal
Endings of eras. Only the sun is constant.

For now.

And it's OK if you feel the need to mourn.
Especially if the scent was sweet and the
Hue more blood than breath.

Yet with the strike of a single match.
Just. like. that. a brand-new hat on a sweet new flesh
Bearing the carriage of some old familiar spirit.
Same warm caress. different, the scent.

All are multifaceted distractions
Of the same illusions we make up as we go.

Go slow.
Touch glass.
Look past.
Into. Self.

Spin Cycle

The pain?
    That's your Self
    Molting

Don't fight it.
Go through it. It's the
Only way to the world waiting
On the other side.

Make the most of it.
Stir your tears into the palette
Of your soul. Mix that shit up.
Imagine your favorite hue.

Blood
Is a primary color.
Like blues.

Ever wonder what keeps
Dreams from coming true?
Cuz the dreaming's being dreamt
On the wrong side of you.

Feels like
Death, don't it?
It is.

The death of
A life you've outgrown.
What do I know?

I got a closet
Full of selves I can't
Be anymore.

Let it spin.

Let it stretch. Let it break
Shake that shit off. This new
Is gonna look good on you.

3

Three

Love Birds

Chained love| ain't. Caged birds
Sing slave hymns.| Whims be sickle.
Free love.| Fly on home.

Meshell

You are bass| drippin'
    From the attic.| Earth's quake.| Blues
    You be herb| gods smoke.

Dysmorphia

Skin deep was never
Only. Razor's edge knows the
Ledge will make you jump.

Wanderlust

Stardust shores.| We are
Infinity in Finite
Flesh| God's wanderlust.

Pretty

He asked, how'd you get
  Them scars? She said these ain't scars
  They highlights, baby.

Th|ink

One day I will write
What I fear most to disclose
And I will not die.

Psyche

Head in the clouds, she's
    Trapped inside a thunderstorm
    Clawing at the sun.

Congo

As we speak| the blood
Dries| the bodies rigor| the
Bullets cool| unseen.

Pilgrims

Greed has no shame. They
Want the land. Call ICE on the
Natives. Steal what's left.

Samsara

Ev'ry headstone is
A Dear John letter. Ev'ry
Birth a making-up.

Four

Impermanence

Breath is all there is.
Even it we must exhale.
Inhale. Now let go.

Solar

You are the sun in
My eyes. When you are around
All else is shadow.

Dawn

She unzip mood. Let
It gather 'round her feet. Step
Out into the light.

Caterpillar

Never stop a child
From chasing butterflies. S|he
Is learning to fly.

Shift

Piece by piece
　The mountain retrieves itself
　　From the stone.

Seed

Love deep enough to
   Draw blood. Strike bone. Keep going
   Plant self in marrow.

Toni

She's cathedral. The
Ink in God's pen. Bleed through. Stain
Glass. Burn cross. Set free.

Zealot

Her lips are God's spell.
   I imagine angels fall
      Every time she speaks.

Alchemy

How you slip through wind
   Though| You be more mountain than
   Air.| Alchemetic soul.

Sanctuary

F all to pieces. It's
OK to do that here. These
Arms are sacred ground.

;

B efore you go, let
    Me beg you to stay. If you
    Must| I'll hold your hand.

Five

Nocturne

And of the night
    Wherein merchants of dreams
    Peddle their wares
To the sleeping
And half-born

Wherein dawn passes
Through corridors of flight
Winged only to the woken
Who seldom venture to the
Marketplace of If
But for trinkets of reflection
To adorn their beloved.

Necklaces of inklings
'Round collar of the selves
Who dream not for they cannot
Afford such reckless squandering
Of time and circumstance.

Yet flock they, to the courtyards
The merchants and the dreamers
The peddlers and the poets of all
That pass-through star and dust

For chance at immortality
Before the clock strikes daylight
Breaking nocturnal spell
Of ever after.

Celeste

A familiar lover,
    The moon slips
        Through my window.

But tonight
There is something different
About her.

She dons the after-glow
Of morning
Rising over me.

And I
Can smell the sun
On her breast as she
Touches me with
The same caress

Leaving levees of his sol
Breaking between my thighs.
And she is so beautiful
I let her sway mood like Delta.

Her glance is an avalanche
Of ... How could you
Move me this way?
Touch me like morning
In the bedroom of night.

Evanescence

If only for the moment
   Let us love. let us be
    The gods we are.

We are but a blink
In the eyes of creation
The sweetest exhale.

If only for the day
Let us pray we stay
Forever sacred.

Recyclable Souls

In the darkness, I cried. Broken.
   And when the blood dried I gathered
   The dust into a satchel.

Came morning, I set out on the road.
Not far had I gone before the wind carried
My way the moans of a girl child crying.

Followed I the sound until I found her naked
Alone in a brush of thorns. Why are you crying, my love?
They broke me, she said. Thighs the purple black
Of a starless night. Where is your mother?
I have none, she whispered. Ashamed.

Reached, I, for satchel while she wept. Collecting her
Tears inside an ink pen gone dry. It was dusk that came
Before the dawn. The sky was falling.

By the blaze of her rage, I trickled the dust from
My darkness into the pen of tears. By the quiver of her fears
I shook until tears swallowed dust back to blood
Into glue we two used to mend the pieces
Of our throw-away souls.

Recyclable, we are
In this second-hand life.

Shadows

I am
   So carefully curated
    My shadow self has
Shadow selves.

I can admit this
Because I have come to
Peace with the wolves
Who hold my Self
Over the fire of revelation.

I nod to the flicker of
The finger puppets of my
Inner children.

They tell
The most captivating stories
Of how it got here,
This self I show
The world.

They understand
And so do not rebel
When I hush them should
Company come.

I am ever vigilant
Over the wolves and children.
I have an image to uphold.

But I have found

My self less and less
Sentinel as the years go by.
Careless even.

Sometimes
I pretend not to see
One of them sneaking past me.
A mouth full of secrets
A pocket full of flames.

Perhaps, I think,
It's better this way.
Helpful, maybe,
To someone else.

Sometimes
I'll even send my regards
As I feed the wolves
Stoke the fire.

Make art
Of shadow
Puppets
Telling
On
Self.

Anima

She is black wings
    Through black night.
    Invisible.

A whisper lost to the wind.
The 'wait. never mind'| of a fading friend.
Unheard.

A single tear| drops.
And adds to the water in which it drowns.
She is savior incapable of saving herself.

She is unanswered prayer
On the lips of saintly sinner.
A god|is. in heathen's skin.

Undiagnosed

Some dreams you body.
  Bury over and over and

Some dreams you worship
Like gods who created you
Like parents who had and then
Forgot you.

Some dreams you chase
Like a carrot at the end of a stick or
That one stuffed unicorn you
Promised your 5-year-old self but

It's trapped inside a vending machine in
Some abandoned amusement park and
You're running out of tokens
Of 'why I do this.'

She thinks it's real
Believes it's alive.

How do you explain stuffed
Unicorns can't really fly
To a kid who rides its wings
Every time you manage a miracle
To slip into that rusted slot.

Some dreams
Are expensive
Make you pawn your soul.

FIVE

Some dreams are cheap
They only cost your life.

Stutter

Betwixt the cool of the quiet
    And the revelry of the passionate
    A spirit is choosing an embryo.
Meticulous the calculated course
Through blue-born veins.

On the edge of yellow, shadows create
Worlds in which to even the odds.
The light has proved elitist and has cast
Off more than it knew it grew.

Somewhere a word sits inside
Abortion clinic waiting anxiously
To purge itself of a meaning
It cannot provide for.

In bio-hazard bag a poem
Is born full term among fragmented
Pieces of the unfinished
And untitled.

Tea Time

Dearest,
    Know that when you call
    You summon all of me.
Not just the sum of the parts
You are comfortable with.

Know that I am compassionate.
That I will silence the shadows for you
But that does not mean
They are not there.

And we can sit in the cozy of kitchen
Talk stories 'round your table of feast
And I, too, may forget they are present
And be as startled as you

Should your shadows
Ask mine to dance
As they slip from quiet of corner
To two-step over your fine China.

Six

Poetry Be Lover

Kissed on forehead
    After hard day's work
        Fragrance enticing … just
Not right now, baby.

Waits
On other side of wall.
I be outside
Even when
I'm not.

Poetry
Be
Lover

Half touched
Longing.
We fuck
On the way to
Something else to do
Right quick.
All day.

I'll be back.

Poetry
Be
Lover

Waking me from sleep.

Talk to me
I'm tired
Talk to me
I'm trying
Talk to me
Don't let me go, baby
Talk to me
But work
Talk to me
I'm dying without you
Talk to me
I'm sorry
Talk to me
C'mere
Talk to me
Let me touch you
Talk to me
Right here
Talk to me
Is where I hurt you
Talk to me
Is where you waited
Talk to me
Is where I left you
Talk to me
Is where you love me
Talk to me
Forgive me?
Yes

Poetry
Be
Lover

Wet in hands
Like feast after famine.

Kiss bruise soul deep.
Keep shadows.

Hold breath when
I don't want it no more
Slip into sighs
I swallow
Like air.

The Sky is a Voyeur

Don't bother discretion.
    Leave your guards where you stand
    And walk away.

None but the sky is watching
None who matter.
I promise.

The wind is a gossip.
Wasted not your efforts on whispers
It will carry them far and wide away

And without regard
To confidence
Or shame.

The sum of our bodies
Each one of us. An antenna the creator
Uses to feel. To taste. To experience
Vibratory frequencies conjured in the dark.

When we touch, we are but vibration
Awaiting the return of echoes
Against our own awaiting
Cell|ves.

The sky is a voyeur.
Don't bother discretion.
Leave your guards where you stand
And walk away.

None but the sky is watching.
None who matter.
I promise.

Lean Not

That time you prayed
    From somewhere under
    Creak of old floorboards

Watching the dogs,
The mice, the fleas
Scurrying mightily
Over you

Nailed down by your
Own understanding.

That time you knew
That God knew
And you were ashamed.

That time you sang
Some song come up from
Depth of sorrow.

Hollowed out
Burrowed through
Let loose from your
Own understanding

Way down under
Them creaking planks.
Tears rolled into ears. Wings
Stretch like breath in chest.

And you knew

That God knew

And you were
Redeemed.

Basket

I've got
    This basket
        Made of arms and
Love and faith.

And I am careful
What I put in this basket
Because I know
How heavy it can get.

Used to be
I'd get greedy
Try to get all I could
In there. But
The road gets rocky
Sometimes.

Hasn't failed yet
All the good stuff falls
Right off the top.

It'll seem like
By the time you get to
Catch your breath

You find you're left
With what all sticks to the
Bottoms of things.

Like shit
And sediment

And soot.

Like regret
And missed opportunities
And fragments of visions
You can't see anymore.

These days
I'm steady with my basket
Real selective too.
Got to make sure what goes into it
Is worth the weight.

I've got this basket
Of arms and love and faith
And I'm carrying it, see
Like my life depends on it.

Familial

When I heard the news
    That I had no mother,
        That my carrier intended me dead,
That an angel saved my life
But could do nothing for my soul,
I packed my things.

Wandered deep into the forest
Of my self. until I came to a clearing
And there I slept. and there I ate
And there I gathered from the night,
Mothers for my self.

I was seed, plucking fruit from trees
When only weeds would feed me.
Toni. Maya. bell. Zora. Nina
I gathered.

Harriet. Fannie. Angela
Come, mama. Come
Ka'ahumanu. Lili'uokalani. Haunani.
I gather. Assata. Jamaica. Octavia.

Take back to center. Billie
Ai. Sapphire. Alice. Audre
Come, mama, talk to me.

I gathered.
Am gathering still.
I am embrya
Building tribe.

Indigenous

It wasn't until I decolonized my mind
    That I realized my body itself had been colonized
    By those I loved since the day I was born.

Sketch

A rms
   Outstretched
     I take me in.
Where has
So much of me
Gone?

I
Remember my Self
Vast and wide.

Steep as ashes
Up swept
In undertow
Of gust.

There
Used to be an ocean
Here.

I swear.

These
Limbs
Are fading.

Fog lights
No match
For rush
Of
Spirits

Crossing
Over and
Back.
And

Sometimes
In subways

I
Look for me
In eyes
Of Windows.

Echoes
Hushed
Then
Swallowed.

I
Take me
In.

What's
Left of me.

These
Dreams
Gushing forth
To
Recede
Quite
Ungracefully.

Kicking
Scratching

Cussing
Begging

All
This flesh

Spilling
Over bones
Pushing
Against
Scars

Who
Are we fooling?
We who?

I
Am
Island.

All I am
Stands
Submerged.

If
No one
Is looking
Who will
See

All
This me
Fading
Away?

Hand Me Down

We grow up on
    Hand-me-downs.

Hand-me-down clothes and
Hand-me-down shoes.
Hand-me-down issues and
Hand-me-down blues.

Hand-me-down me.
Patchwork prodigy in
Latchkey conditions.
Threadbare restrictions and
Re-stitched religions.

Hand-me-down addictions
Hand in hand with
Hand-me-down scars.
Hand-me-down tomorrows
Held back by
Hand-me-down bars.

Hand me down a hook.
Bout to catch me a star.
What's new?

Glue

A sheltered child from a sheltered home
    Crossed the tracks one day.

It's like that sometimes, the gutter
Calls the sympathists from their embroidered sheets
To dabble on a bugged-out mattress or cardboard box.

Caught me half bite through my Slim Jim
Struck up a conversation.

They do that sometimes, the tourists
Interrupt sacred shit
Like survival
With their curiosity fetishes.

How do you all do it?
Asked the adventurist.

I swallow

It's the glue
The glue?
Yeah, the glue.

You know?
Shit gets broken, you glue it, right?
Or maybe you
Don't know.

Where you from, shit breaks
You throw it away, right?

SIX

Yes, she says. kind of surprised
Surprised I spoke, or surprised I ain't robbed her yet
Who knows. But whatever.

I chew.

But I'm talking about people, not things
how do you people stay so strong
I mean.. you know.. in all this... this...

I swallow.

Two things, Dora...
First, I was talkin' about people.
Somebody gets broken in your
Shiny house what do you do?
Throw that motherfucker into a
Pill bottle or psyche ward, right?

Or worse. you let 'em throw themselves
Away across the tracks
Or over a blade or up a bullet.
Or into the arms of a black man.
Or this... This... Shit.
Shit is the word you were lookin' for.

Second, it's the glue.
When you're used to getting broken
You learn how to piece yourself together.
But of course, you wouldn't know that
I can tell your smile ain't got no cracks.

This hurt her feelings.
I feel bad.
Shit,

She ain't got no glue.

Seven

Splendid

Splendid is the night
No bombs fall. The moment is
Fleeting. Come| give thanks.

Tomorrow we will
Gather the pieces of the
Dead. Re|member them

As they were| Smiling.
They say the world is watching
Yet it is silent.

Our prayers seem to
Go no higher than our heads| Then
Shatter at our feet.

There is no food in
The pots| But there is shelter
Here in the rubble

Of all we used to
Know.| The air has turned our tears
To trails from our eyes

To our mouths. We speak
low| Choose carefully our words
Each may be our last.

Splendid is the night
No bombs fall.| The moment is
fleeting. Come|give thanks.

Water Log

The ship is sinking
    And we are trying to patch
    The holes with duct tape

But there ain't enough
To go around, see? Congo,
Palestine, Sonya.

The ship is sinking
But we're fighting over who
The captain will be.

The holes are getting
Bigger. Genocide, famine
Rape as a weapon.

The ship is shrinking
Get yo hand out my pocket!
We shout to drown sound

Of all the bodies
Falling overboard. Babies
Swallowing water.

There are no life vests
Here. They're on the yacht ahead
And they can't hear us

Over their campaigns--
Propaganda. Meanwhile, we
Capsize the dinghy.

Hush

I wrote a senryu
Yesterday. It was about
Death. I buried it.

Suddenly aware
Hyper-vigilant of the
Power in our words.

Like a child playing
With fire in her mother's
House. Almost found out.

Stuffed the poem under
A rug. Deleted it from
The ether as if

Death would not come to
Those who say not its name. Like
That shit ever worked.

I wrote a senryu
Yesterday. For the fallen
And the slain. It read

Death is a thief who
Stalks in broad day. Look out. Here
Comes the smash-and-grab

Now hold breath. Pray for
A blessed mortality. Make
Peace with God within.

Flesh Envy

I claim this beauty
    This skin stretched taut over drum.
    Only I can hear.

The wolves outside my
Window. They are drawn to the
Moonlight in my fire.

I claim this valley.
Thighs wrap 'round mountains. Rivers
Trickle. Rush. Break dam.

Who are we who are
Here? Obsessions of Gods with
Flesh envy. They are

Rings. I am Saturn.
I claim this space. Stardust on
Lips. Andromeda.

I claim this breath. Breathe.
Feel dirt 'neath feet. Breeze on neck.
See wolves lick teeth. Smile.

Eight

Glitch

Right now
>There are lovers loving
>>Bombs dropping
>
>Children playing
>Bullets shredding

Lives apart.

Stitched together.

Piecemeal
Peace feel
Heavy sometimes
Like old wounds on
New wishes.

Right now
Rage is a baby
Love left alone
In a hot car
For a fix
Or
Whatever.

Silence is a lullaby
In a war zone
Bordered on all sides
By happy hours.

Right now
Bad grammar

Is the least of concerns
In life sentences.
Dis,traction
Is a misplaced ! mark.

I have no gift to give.
Save your trinkets.
No cents in bartering
Bullshit. We are
Fertile. What grows here
Dies here. Like us
Right now.

40/Seven

The dream is burning.
    These are not our father's
    Puppeteers.

There is no curtain.
We are fucked on full display
For the world to see.

We are the dumb girl
In that horror porn who
Followed the apps
Into the woods

Where X, Meta, & Amazon
Waited to run a train on
What was left of our ignorance.

Oh, we thought
They were our friends?
Plot twist.

Our greatest enemies
Rode shotgun all along.
Right here in the palms
Of our greedy lil hands.

II

Knock, knock

Who's there?
ICE.

III

From my window
I can see the neighbor's children
Playing in the crystal rays
Of the winter sun.

I think of my granddaughter
What world have we unleashed
On her. On them?

My mother raised
An obedient child. A
Quiet witness to
The world.

I pray my daughter
Raises a hellion. Because
Fuck these adults.

I pray she rages
I pray they all rage
Against the evil that is
This machine devouring
Everything In its path.

IV

May the lead
In our chambers
Pierce the hearts
Of our enemies.

lowercase gods

and we
with our lowercase gods
and uppercase egos,

where shall we go?
when the dust settles?
when the blood clots?

our children lay scattered
in the fields we've abandoned.
so, too, our elders

they burn
hatred for the cowardice
of their heroes

we cut our eyes
at the midday sun
who turns it's back

on our shame.
it is here on the mountaintop
our deepest valleys lay.

Send Them

Where are the troops
    Come from elsewhere
        Sent by some righteous other
To save us from the tyranny
Of our government?

Unreported

I dreamt once of an invisible storm
    A rare dream in greyscale

Of a town just off the freeway
That echoed of emptiness and approaching

Streets abandoned of its people
Windows boarded for protection
From a chaos all could feel but none could see.

As I walked the hollow
The earth trembled.
The sky roared.

Winds swept through the space between
A rage untethered. Inconsolable

But looking out through window of eye
One could deny the terror
Experienced by spirit alone.

Dreamt I of a storm one night
One without witness
Save for the soul

Wading through weather
And churning undertow
Just beneath the skin.

Armageddon

It was a
    Wednesday mornin' or a
    Friday afternoon

On my way to work
When I heard the boom
Looked to the sky
And I saw a shroom
Of smoke and fire
Like a devil's bloom.

An Armageddon

There were sisters cryin'
And brothers runnin'
And babies fallin'
Like shells from guns.

An Armageddon

Got out of my truck
And the earth was spinnin'
And the trees were snappin'
And the blood was spillin'
And the birds were slingin'
From the arms of the wind.

An Armageddon

And I fell to my knees
I said help me, lord

EIGHT

I know I ain't been faithful
But can I get on board

It is an Armageddon

But the lord was silent
And my heart grew quiet
Cuz all the gods and demons
Had minds like mine. It's
Like lookin' for signs
Blinded by time

In this Armageddon

And we swing from beliefs
Like corpses from roots.
And we see with our eyes
But don't believe the proof
That the house was burnin'
While we were raisin' the roof

To Armageddon.

Surviving the Night

Last night
   I was Earth
      Quaking
Trembling
Holding breath.

Tears
Lava
Seeping through
Fissures
Of a breaking me.

Last night
She was Heaven
Reaching through dark
Down and in
Finding
Pulling
Holding
On.

As the mountain
I am turn mud
Slide 'way
Leave hollow
Soundless.

Last night
The only night
For miles.

EIGHT

Trickle blue black
Over brown bodies
Rivers coursing
From bend in eye
'Round ring fingers.

And me
Only Earth
Held tight

To a Heaven
Believing me
Redeemable.

Courtship

I took her
   To the middle of an
     Abandoned scrap yard
Littered with blooms of Orchids. Plumeria.

Reeking with the stench of
Gardenias projectile dreaming
Beneath stars swinging
From velvet nooses.

I laid my cloak across the runoff
Of a phosphorescent stream receding against itself until
We reached the jagged banks
Of an island afloat in the middle of a
Forest buried in the center of a desert
Upon which lie an old pine box.

Open it, I said to her
She did. At which the lid
Turned to wings of smoke and shadow,
Flying away in the up-spiraled winds.

In her eyes were reflections of
The lives of light in all emissions of existence
Shimmering. Blazing. Fading
Gone.

What do you see?
I asked, becoming faint as
Sound in hollow of hourglass.

Your heart, she replied
Without looking back;
Letting her garments fall
In ripples around her feet
As she climbed inside.
The old pine box.

Wake

The day you died
    The stars spoke the story
    Of how you came
Kicking and screaming
Out of the portal of flesh.

Of how they pulled you
Headfirst from the womb of the moon.
Of how they fell silent at your silence
Once on the other side. Of how they
Thought you stillborn until the sun hit you
And you cried your first breath.

One day they'll ask you
How much you remember
About the day you died.

Will you tell them we mourned you?
Will you tell them we could not protect you?
Will you tell them we loved you?
That we wailed your name?

Will you recall what we called you
Before you died to be born
Among the stars?

9
Nine

Fly

I Am breath
Stroking through a
Water-colored sky.

Rainbow ripples trail
The tales of who I've been
On other side of skin.

No|thing exists
Until I believe it.

Breath
Stroke
Breath
Stroke

Fly.

Salt

We make love in deserts
    Miles from seas and yet
    The salt in the sweat between us
Connects us to unseen oceans.

There is something sacred here
Where motions ebb and flow.
Where tides, conjured between breadth
And breath, manifest the same substance
Present in the undertows that pulled
Our ancestors to the bottoms of passages
We have been fucking to surface from.

We are cycles circling sacred triangles
Denied entry by the very baptisms
Promising our deliverance.

Don't cry, my love, but if you must
I will swallow the burdens your eyes can no longer hold
Get carried away through the hollow
Of your twice-sold soul.

Become a river to
An ocean we have loved
Into existence but
Have yet to see.

I can hear us
There in the shells of our empty selves
Generations of waves crashing back to us
Along the sanctified shores of our longing

Because

There is something holy in the sweat
That envelopes the tears
That connects our desert
To an unseen sea.

Billie

Billie Holiday died
    In the bottom of a bottle
      Encapsulated
In the tomb of a pill.

And we

Mesmerized
By the seduction
Of her moans,

Touched ourselves
To the slow whine
Of her suicide.

Orbit

There is a place
    Inside depression
        Wide as all outside.

There is no sensation here.

No thought.
No touch.
No feel.

It is like orbiting
Your own humanity

Your return is
Neither processed
Nor pending.

You're a satellite
Able only to exchange intel
But not emotion for
Emotion is indigenous
And you are foreign matter.

From this place
One can almost long
For the tears of drowning.

Conjure the pull of current.
The plight of fight
The sweet, sweet sweep
Of undertow.

Passport

At the gates of Introspection
    I am forced to leave my words behind.

Vernacular is sub specie of external habitation
And prone to invasive contagions.

Unable to clear my thoughts, I am escorted
To quarantine, where I am made to
Disrobe my Self of sound and

Am passed through a series of silent showers
Until all residue of rhetoric is washed loose.

I tell you this now
Because I may not see you again
And if I do, I may not remember your name.

Journeys to Introspection can do that
Separate Futures from Pasts.

Illusion

We Search the see's
    For sanctuary.
Blind to the fact

That's even as
We seek, we are grains
Of sand slipping

From beneath the feet
Of we who think we islands
In ocean of discontent.

New hearts
Old scars. Open wounds of
Self-inflicted tragedies.

We are
Laughable. And yet
Love is not
Amused.

Old Shit

Little girls
    Little boys
        Devastated
By molestation
Uncles, babysitters, relations.

Grow up fighting demons
Unprecedented, or so they think.
Secrets, shame. Don't tell yo moms.

Fight world
Kill selves
Fuck God.

Tell somebody
Stranger, lover, friend
Anybody.

Throw weight from shoulder
Find relief in bottle bottoms
Sit next to Ol Man Murphy
Sista Shug at the barrio bar
Chit chat.

Spill beans over Grey Goose.
Feel earth shake at confession
My uncle, father, priest…
touched me.

Ol Man Murphy,
Sista Shug say

Shit! You too?

And just like that
Shame fall away.
That's life, they say.

Turn up
Fall down.
Is it really?

Wake up in mornin'
Demons ain't changed
Only now, they got company.

Night Sweats

She dreams of nightmares
    Life is a merciless death.

There's a baby in the closet
Swinging from a leather strap.
Belt buckle tattoo burned into its neck.
A teething ring lodged in its throat.

There's a calico in the window
Enviously watching alley strays
Foraging for fish eyes.

Faceless ghosts grab at barbed feet.
She is running and out of reach.

She dreams of nightmares
Life is a merciless death.

There's a rat in the toilet
Maggots feast on cyanide cadaver.
Poisoned, they convulse
On fecal rafts.

Her lips. Are blue.
Her face. Is gray.
Her hair. Is white.
Her nails. Are black.

Her dreams are
Technicolor horror flicks.

She is trying to fly but can't
The sky is crashing.
She is running through mushroom clouds.
Arms flapping off a sudden cliff.

There's a rumor at the bottom
She is racing to the truth.

She dreams of nightmares
Life is a merciless de--

Therapy

I watch her scribble
    Teary-eyed
      Over the bodies I've
Coughed up.

She feels accomplished
I've spilled my guts.

But she don't know
'Bout the corpse
I hold in the crevice
Of my cheek.

It's rancid.
Spitting it out
Is always a risk.

But if I
Play this right
I can take it
To my grave.

Spit it on God.
Demand justice
For what s|he allowed
To happen
On he|r watch.

She's talking... again.
Wants to know
How this makes me feel.

15 minutes.
The corpse is stirring.
Death is an acquired
Taste.

10
Ten

Rosario

Tears fall
    Syncopated
       Sound of wind
Chimes.

Child come
From blood of Lono,
God of harvest.

Growing garden
In land of Smiths
Washingtons
Martinez.

My mother
Has a tombstone
With an ocean view
Up Holualoa way.

My sisters gather
Pikake, Plumeria
Drape Maili over
Nameplate.

Rosario
Grew Rose gardens
Orchids. Anthuriums
Food. Children.
Love.

There is a photo of her

TEN

In the long green hallway
Of my memory. Sepia
Goddess in house dress
Floating barefoot over
Bones of ancestors
Planting breath.

She sees me
Crying. Reaching
For hem of fog and mist.
Lips smiling. Eyes
A sky of flashbacks.

Don't cry
for me.

There is an hourglass
In her right hand. A conch
In the other. She tilts her
Head in the direction
Of my children.

Ku'u Home.

She drifts. I am rising.
She drifts. I am flying.
She drifts. I am home.

Ku'ulei

There are things
    they don't tell you you'll miss
        When you move from the islands
To the city.

Like stars
And earth
And the innocence
In your own skin.

Firefly

We are fireflies in midday sky.
    Born this very dawn.
        Glorious, we find the sun
Iridescent through our wings.

We hide and seek ourselves
Beneath every falling leaf
And wind-swept grocer's bag.
Tag. Red light. Go.

The street lights sing no song
And so we know not what to make
Of the sudden trail of beams we
Are unable to lose in the night.

Noteworthy

It's true
   What they say about
   Writers and windows
We watch the world
Like most watch television.

Entranced sometimes
Sometimes absent-minded
But we watch
For hours on end.

The cities. The rivers.
Mountains. Sea. Alleyways.
Dirt roads. Life contained
Therein.

Absorb. Digest. Reflect.

We
Like to call ourselves
Writing about it
That part's not true.

I don't believe it, anyway

I do believe
That there at the window
We become canvas
Page. Paper napkin.

A notebook in the hands

TEN

Of Gods
Who, when inspired
Turn their gaze to us.

Open us up
Scribe across the breadth
Of our spirits
Their passing muse.

And they are human, the Gods
In nature. One day we be masterpiece
The next, scratch paper.

Sometimes
They don't write anything at all
Just stare at us staring.

We, blank pages
Propped 'gainst window frame
Waiting to be transformed
Into something

Noteworthy.

Deserts

Sweeping stretches of sand and dirt
   Where grass and tree refuse to grow
     Naked hollows where the earth whispers
I am enough.

Gabriel

Had warrants
    The kind paying your tickets
    Don't scrub clean.

Asked me for a ride
To the grocery store.

Passed up the chicken breast
and pork chops.
Took me to the
Bagged parts.

Feet
Necks
Beaks
Tongues

Said
This watchu you call
Ends meeting.

Gabriel
Called me friend
Wanted to hang out
With a woman
He wouldn't touch.

Wanted to know
What that's like
Knowing a woman
Not touching her.

Gabriel
Lived in a room
Above his uncle's shop
Sloped floor. Old stove
Fed belly. Kept Bible
In one hand
Clip. in the other.

Gabriel
Be gone now
Ten leagues
Under radar.

Gabriel
Be that poem
You gotta write
From the inside
Out.

This Moment

My heart
    I tell you now
        What you already know.

Depression
Returns.
Anxiety
Remains.

They must.

For they are
Atmosphere
And you
Are Earth.

Where thunder ebbs
Rainbows rush.
Lightning strikes reveal
What hides within the dark
Nights of our soul.

Blue now, is the sky.

Play.
Laugh.
Rejoice.

Say to the sun
I have missed you.
Come.

Wash over me
Your sacred rays.
Baptize me in
Your warm embrace.

Dear heart
I tell you now
Lick the tear and
Savor the smile.

You are Earth
All else
Is atmosphere.

Mercy

Is the balm in the petals
   Of memories

After

The thorns of life have
Had their way.

Reflection

For we who have followed the hollow
    Of our pens long enough to know there is
        No fanfare for the poet. No entourage
For the writer. Not really.

Not until the universe has been satisfied
By the blood of our solitude.
Then, only the whisper of the wind
Will prove sincere enough hear.

For only the air we breathe will
Truly know the sacrifices made
By our hearts.

After the mics have been silenced.
After more books have been shelved than peddled.
It is in silence, and it is alone that we succumb
To the calling that beckoned us out of
Our mothers' wombs.

It is after the accolades have quieted that the wise ones
Will gather at the feet of the elders who do not shout,
But speak gently and effortlessly the winds
Beneath our flailing wings, that we may
Continue to stay the course of our solitary flights.

Eleven

Beloved (For Toni)

She was
    Astonishingly loved
        And so we did not wait
Until she died to give her
Her flowers.

And now
All we have to give her
Are pieces of the pieces
Of ourselves she alone
Has planted.

She was in this world
But not of it
Her extraterrestrial sight
Embedded in us the insight
Of a greater understanding

Of what it's like to walk
Through walls and realms.
Hers was more than a passport
She had dual citizenship.

She apologized not.
She bit her tongue not.
Where we saw blood
She showed us the source.

Where we saw angels
She ran her words over
Our own shoulder blades

And said, these are
Your wings,
Too.

They called her an author.
But we who have been born again
In the womb of her wisdom
Know better.

For she did not write
As much as she birthed.
She did not speak
As much as she channeled.

She was our ladder
To the other side and
There are none among us
Who have not been elevated
By the power in her rungs.

See Unheard

I Was child
Woven
Into hem
Of my mother's
Skirt.

Seen
Unheard
While kupuna
Talked stories
Of spirits
And gods
And ether
And earth.

I
Swayed
At my mother's knees
En route to prayers
And blessings
Of houses
Haunted
By faith.

Watched
Offerings placed
On altars. Held breath
Waiting to see what spirit
Would come for them. And
In what form they
Would come.

ELEVEN

Sometimes I'd
Fall asleep to the
Mele of kahuna
To the holy lullabies
Rocking gently
The evil from
Sacred babies.

I
Was baby
Who spoke
The name of
Pele before I
Knew of Jesus

A
Baby
Protected
By aumakua
Before salvation
Was market
Cornered by
Churches.

I am
Here. Still

A thread in my mother's hem.
Swaying through paths
Carved long before
Redemption was road
Hinged from stop sign.

Whitney

You are the diamond they
 Tried to turn to rock, star.
 Cosmic goddess crushed
Through groove of 45.

Smile for me, Whitney.

That smile that makes
Blind men look twice and
Straight girls cut eyes at
The silk in your sighs.

You are beauty so deep,
Seas ripple in half tide to catch
Glimpse of your stride on the
Off shores of our pride.

And it makes no sense
To see you in past tense when
The presence of these tears
Seep futuristic.

You are rising as we speak.
Eternal light in bedroom eye
Of a mourning sky.

Solace

T|here is something
    Godly in he|r tears.
    Some wordless magic
In the wet.

Like when sky slice self
To bleed pon arid ground.

Or when sea come feel a weh
'Bout always being on the bottom
And wrestle cloud cover
Off from over it.

Some w|here in the tussle
God send optigasmic shudder.
Thunder come from
Cloud|less eye.

T|here is something
Godly in he|r tears.
Some wordless magic
In the wet.

Forecast

Weatherman
    Issues a
        Freezing fog
Advisory.

Conjures images
of walking through
glass shadows.

Fragile,
shattered.

Breathe
Cross pane
Of exhale.

Life
Is an inhale
Spilled
Down flight
Of chest.

A wind chime
Dangling
In the stare
Between us.

I Can

Count twice on both hands
    The years since the last one moved me.

Love has been for me a train of thought
Lovers board and disembark
According to my interest in continuing
The itinerary of set tracks.

Don't tell my heart.
It truly believed it was
Doing something.

I apologize to my tongue
For all the times I made it atone
For my body's refusal to play it's part
In whatever script my mind
Had written at the time.

I can

Say this now
Because

I can

Forgive my self the bodies
Strewn along the traveled
Paths. and

I can

Forgive my self
The hearts. Theirs
And mine.
And

I can

Count once on one finger
The times I've known my self enough
To be moved
Again.

Undistorted

True love
    Is the mirror through which you witness
    Everything you knew you were,
But lesser loves could never see.

It is the eyes
Which do not distort but rather
Enhance who you are. And who you are
Is always enough.

No matter
How much or how little
You have become.

Wordlessness

I have a poem
   About depression.
   I am wanting
To share it

To help or
To hold or
To sit beside
The person
Who is suffering
Right now.

It's an honest poem
Describing what being in
The throes of a depressive
Episode feels like.

I believe firmly
That articulation
Liberates.

If one can find the words
To describe exactly what
They're feeling, they can
Be set free.

If a person is feeling
A thing vastly bigger
Than they are, but are
Not able to Express
What that thing is,

ELEVEN

If they are not able to
Carve its form
Or sketch its face or
Imitate the sound of it,
It is akin to being imprisoned
By that very thing.

And if you are
In that kind of prison
The words of someone else
Who has been through
That experience,

Saw for themselves the
Thing you cannot describe,
The very words, the very
Key that set them free
Can also liberate you.

I know
There is somebody
Battling somewhere
With a pain they
Cannot describe

And I have a poem
That may keep you
Company

But my own depression
Will not let me reach for it.
I'm too heavy to move

Still,

I wanted to sit beside
That hurting someone
Even if it is in
Wordlessness.

Misnomer

Forgive us our thorns.
    What was meant to behold
        Gently in our hearts
We snatched with our hands
And when we bled
We wept in pain
And called it love.

The Gardener

I am no expert on Love
   But I know this one thing
   It is not the flower.

Love never lasts
With flower pickers.
Only gardeners know
How to keep it alive.

Habitually we portray images
Of pretty little petals.
Smiling faces.
Warm embraces.

Understandably
Who wouldn't be proud
Of such an enchanting thing.
But the kiss is only
The flower.

We seldom see
The thorns.
The roots.
The wilting leaves.

We should. All of it.

That we may understand
What Love really looks like
When we encounter it's
Possibility.

ELEVEN

The thorns, the arguments.
The issues. Insecurities.
Hurtful things when held
Too tightly out of fear
Of having it slip away.

The roots, watered by
Tears and sweat and blood.
How they grow. Deeper. Stronger
Or rot from over-trying

The wilting leaves.
Old selves shed to make
Room for new and stronger
Versions. Hybrids of compromise.

There is a difference between
One who is willing to get their hands dirty
To kneel and to nurture what they
Cannot yet see but wholly believe in.

And those who've no patience
For such things. Who just want the pretty
Who gather only the petals to lay across beds
Which will inevitably become fields
For the dying and fading away.

Love is Not the Flower
It is the whole of the being.
One does not pick Love
One must grow it.

Twelve

Crush

I want to touch you with new hands
    These old ones are dirty with the work
       It took to get here

I want to speak to you in a new tongue.
You have rendered every syllable of accumulated language
No more than babble|on the scrolls of outdated
Philosophies regarding god particles caught in the
Teeth of love.

I want to hear you with new ears
You are an instrumental I find myself
Writing to across every clean slate
And graffitied cathedral.

I am a break-beat
In your symphony.
A beat-box
To your falsetto.

Is Love

To behold me
    Whilst I am light,
        Shimmering across the ripples
Of a golden sea,
Is lovely.

To wade waist-deep
Through muck of swamp,
To hold breath and submerge,
Eyes open.

To fetch me from sediment of soot
And pull me from the illusion
That I am light
Shimmering across the ripples
Of a golden sea

So that I may be light
Shimmering across the ripples
Of a golden sea,
Is Love.

Songs II

Ballads dangle pearls from earlobes.
    I am entranced by scent of sonnets
        Left like memories in our sheets.

Last night's last flight left us red-eyed
In the afterglow of sunrise. We
Kiss between hello and goodbye
For lifetimes

Are made of these...
Breath held moments. these
'Just one' moments. These...

If the devil won't, surely God
Condones it. She took the fuck from
My waist. it's better this way.

I love deeper than I
Fuck. come harder than I leave
When staying is the object.

She is muse through instrumental.
Hypnotic strobe. Rhythmic band of bangles
Pulsing Soca symphony against drum of head
Board in speakless composition.

Lay Me Down

Stand behind me
   Before this mirror of life
      Cup these hips twice anointed by birth.
  Whisper breath through breast
  Heavy fullness of heart and soul.

Run your fingers
Through these thoughts
Set them free, unchain me
From imagined confines.

Let this cloak of dreams
Fall between us
Let every curve and bend
Of this body succumb.

Lay me down

Find your way
Through these rivers
Take your time
Through these mountains.

If I am earth
Be you atmosphere
A storm raging
A gentle breeze
Ever over me.

Lay me down

TWELVE

You are a seed planted
Push up and through me
Seek sun, rise moon
Let touch bloom mercy
Over hills and valleys.

I am ocean
Reflecting sky of you
A tide rising
Back to your horizon.

Lay me down

Swallow me.
Speak my name.
Whisper prayer.
I long to believe.

I bow before you,
A desert outstretched.
You are scent of rain approaching
Find me succulent.

Lay me down

Tempest

We made love through the storm
    Heaven hurled itself at our window
    Leaving tears of angels to stream
Iridescent droplets down sheer of curtain.

The wind gathered 'round her waist.
And I, gathered in her waist, conjured sound
From music sheets of linen.
Moaned Simone to Coltrane
Until the moon came
Slipping from nocturne.

Tumbling through arch of vertebrae.
An owl from the rapt of Sappho.
Winged apparition
Loosed from channel.

The storm, it passed
The sky, it dried
But I am still gathered,
A song in her waist.

Love Note

I keep
    Our last kiss in my pocket
    A tenderly scribbled love note
Worn by the longing of retrieval.

Roll of tongues imprinted.
Fingerprints.
Thumbed through.
Skimmed.

In the dim light of remembrance
You are my favorite sonnet.
I memorize you
My four-letter alphabet.

Teach you
To my children
That they may learn
What it is to be loved
Beyond a mother's prayer.

I wear
Your pheromone
Behind each earlobe,
Across each wrist.

Don you
Like my Sunday best
On Wednesday mornings
When the world is all
But void of divinity.

Yours is the voice I reply to
When all by my self.
Crazy.

I am that apparition
Beneath crescent moon.
Howling,
neck outstretched.
Wind through tuft of cloak.

Empress
Of palace inhabited
By none

But the echo
Of a love note
Written
By unseen
Hands.

Honey

I'd heard
    The word
        Before.

Honey

Like accent from one who
Come from a garden in some far-off place
I'd never afford to go. or. ever be
Let in.

Honey

Rich.
Sweet…
Too sweet.

Like the mom
From 'Leave it to Beaver'.
'Oh, Ward'- she'd sigh. My
Mom never sighed like that.

If my dad came
Off the cuff,
She'd cut her eyes
Like so. No

Honey.

I come from
Babe and

Ma and
Daddy.

Where babe was in bed by eight
And Ma called Daddy Daddy in a way that
Made him feel like a man, not a buck.

Honey

Come from the other side of tracks.
Over where Sweetheart and Darling be.
Up by the boutiques and teacups like

Honey

Then she came along.
And called me

Honey

Felt like I was in an interracial relationship.
Not of skin but of spirit. Like
What was she doing in my neighborhood?

Where sisters be Sistahs
And brothers be Brah and
The idolized among us had
Comrades for lovers.

Honey

Sweet. soft...
Natural like breeze.
She called me

Honey

I let it flutter round inner ear.
Slide under collarbone.
Settle in heart.

Honey

So this is what the garden's like

Honey

Like morning dew in midday heat

Honey

Let it dance up exhale
and
roll off tongue.

Honey

I like it
Here.

Prey

She
   Speaks a velvet web.
   Captivates me.
Renders my wings
Immobile.

And I
Dazzled by
The shimmer
In her eyes
Succumb

To the silk of her
Touch
The sugar in her
Smile.

If I
Am to be devoured
Let it be like this.
Let it be

Just
Like
This.

And let her
Find me a most
Unforgettable
Capture.

Let

And she confessed
    Love's caress too soft
      To be felt through
Armor.

Let your defenses
Fall away. Your shield
Serves only to deflect that
Which may resurrect you.

And should you rise
Like life toward the warmth
Of the sun. Speak kindly.
Touch softly.

Be love.
It is at once the least you
Could do. and the most
You can be.

Butterfly

She flutters.
    Stopping only for a moment
        No longer than the span of breath
    No longer than a notion's caress.
A memory at best.

Just long enough to imprint upon the mind
A framed capture.
A paned window
Through which she may flutter
Forevermore.

Dragonfly

I want to travel
    Your dark passages and
    Illuminated corridors.

I want to learn from you
All that the world has hidden from me
Because it could only live freely in you.

I promise to humble my self
To listen more than I speak
Arms wide open
To give more than receive.

Your scent is a song
On the wings of dragonflies
And I am ever only a child
Chasing you through fields of dreams.

I am soft here. For you.
You speak and I become sonnet
I have lost my rage
Somewhere in your soliloquy

Someone came and stole
The wand from my tongue.
I won't need it where I'm going
If you let me.

12

Weave for me a shadow
    Drape it 'round my neck
    Let it fall like hush o'er the
Meter of my prose.

    Lick midnight
    From the dawn
    Of thigh, then tell me
    How well I work the dark.

A native of the islands of Hawaii, Journey is a daughter to Queen Lili'uokalani living in the black skin of the enslaved ancestors; she is a daughter to Harriet Tubman. Both their lives can be found in the bold pain, rage, resiliency, and strength of her words. Her work is quiet and calculating. She observes the world and every detail in it. She is an investigator. A reporter. A griot.

E. Nina Jay
Poet/Activist

www.ingramcontent.com/pod-product-compliance
Lightning Source LLC
Chambersburg PA
CBHW070426010526
44118CB00014B/1924